The Museum of Modern Art
New York

ABC

Florence Cassen Mayers

Harry N. Abrams, Inc.
Publishers
New York

For my children, Lela and Dara, and my husband, Bob,
and for my mother

Editor: Sheila Franklin
Designer: Florence Cassen Mayers

Library of Congress Catalog Card Number: 86–70407
ISBN 0–8109–1849–8 (Abrams)
ISBN 0–87070–280–7 (Museum of Modern Art)

Design copyright © 1986 Florence Cassen Mayers

Times Mirror Books

Printed and bound in Japan

Introduction

This ABC is unique and beautiful because each letter of the alphabet is illustrated with a painting, sculpture, or design from the extraordinary collection of The Museum of Modern Art, New York.

The book has been designed to appeal to children of all ages. For the preschool child, it provides a novel way to learn the alphabet; for the older child, it is a wonderful treasury of modern-art masterpieces. Preschool children turning the pages of this book will immediately recognize "Goat" for G, "House" for H, "Moon" for M. They need not know that these are works by Picasso, Edward Hopper, or Rousseau in order to delight in and enjoy them. Older children, just becoming aware of art and museums, will find in this a true first artbook, an exciting way to get a glimpse of modern art. Through the images on these pages, art becomes accessible and fun. Children will be fascinated to discover that things as friendly and familiar as bathrobes, kitchens, and cheeseburgers or as varied and interesting as automobiles and flags can all be part of a museum collection.

If you live near the Museum, take this book along as a guide the next time you visit with your children. Encourage them to search for their favorite objects, to hunt for Matisse's *Dance*, for example, or Van Gogh's *Starry Night*. Soon your children will be guiding you.

What more wonderful way could there possibly be for a child to learn the ABCs of language *and* art than through this book and this collection?

Aa

Automobile

Pinin Farina
Cisitalia "202" GT Car
1946. Aluminum body, 4'1" x 4'10" x 12'5"
Manufacturer: Carrozzeria Pininfarina S.p.A.,
Italy
Gift of the manufacturer

Bb

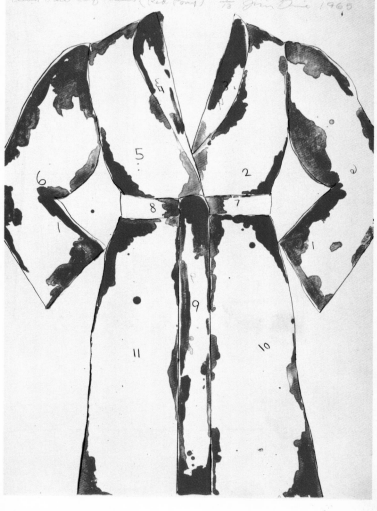

Bathrobe

Jim Dine
Eleven Part Self-Portrait (Red Pony)
1965. Lithograph, printed in color, 39¾ x 29⅝"
Gift of the Celeste and Armand
Bartos Foundation

Cc

Cheeseburgers

Claes Oldenburg
*Two Cheeseburgers with Everything
(Dual Hamburgers)*
1962. Burlap soaked in plaster, painted
with enamel, 7 x 14¾ x 8⅝"
Philip Johnson Fund

Dd

Dance

Henri Matisse
Dance (first version)
1909. Oil on canvas, 8'6½" x 12'9½"
Gift of Nelson A. Rockefeller in honor
of Alfred H. Barr, Jr.

Ee

Elephant

Alexander Calder
Elephant Chair with Lamp
1928. Galvanized sheet steel, iron wire,
lead, cloth, and painted-paper construction,
7⅞ x 3½ x 4⅛"
Gift of the artist

Ff

Flag

Flowers

Jasper Johns
Flag
1955. Encaustic, oil, and collage
on canvas, 42½ x 60⅝"
Gift of Philip Johnson in honor of
Alfred H. Barr, Jr.

Odilon Redon
Vase of Flowers
1914. Pastel on paper, 28¾ x 21⅛"
Gift of William S. Paley

Goat

Pablo Picasso
She-Goat
1950 (cast 1952). Bronze, after found objects,
47⅝ x 56⅜ x 27¾"; at base, 41⅛ x 28⅛"
Mrs. Simon Guggenheim Fund

Hh

House

Edward Hopper
House by the Railroad
1925. Oil on canvas, 24 x 29"
Given anonymously in 1930 by
Stephen C. Clark

Ii

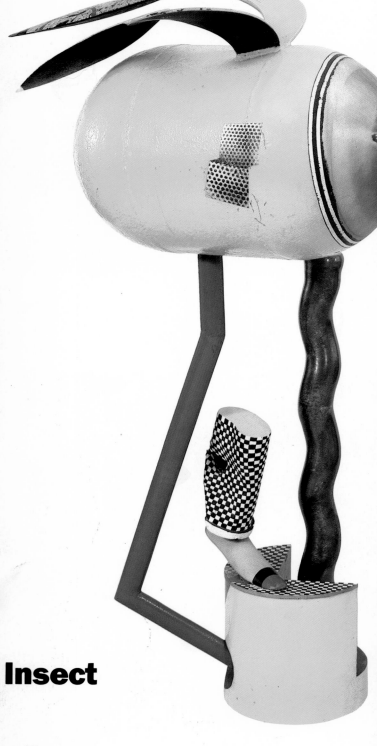

Insect

Robert Hudson
Fat Knat
1964. Painted metal construction,
55⅛ x 17½ x 53⅞"
Fractional gift of Charles Cowles

Jj

Jewel box

Joseph Cornell
Taglioni's Jewel Casket
1940. Wood box containing glass ice
cubes, jewelry, etc., 4¾ x 11⅞ x 8¼"
Gift of James Thrall Soby

Kk

Kitchen

Tom Wesselmann
Still Life Painting, 30
1963. Assemblage: oil, enamel, and
synthetic polymer paint on composition board
with collage of printed advertisements, plastic
artificial flowers, refrigerator door, plastic
replicas of 7-Up bottles, glazed and framed
color reproduction, and stamped metal,
48½ x 66 x 4"
Gift of Philip Johnson

Ll

Lion

Henri Rousseau
The Sleeping Gypsy
1897. Oil on canvas, 51" x 6'7"
Gift of Mrs. Simon Guggenheim

Mm

Moon

Nn

Night

Vincent van Gogh
The Starry Night
1889. Oil on canvas, 29 x 36¼"
Acquired through the Lillie P. Bliss Bequest

Oo

Ocean

Milton Avery
Sea Grasses and Blue Sea
1958. Oil on canvas, 60⅛" x 6'⅜"
Gift of friends of the artist

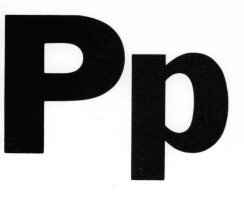

Pp

Plate

Pot

Robert Venturi
"Notebook" Plate
1984. Glazed porcelain, 1¼" high;
diameter at rim, 12¹⁄₁₆"
Manufacturer: Swid Powell, U.S.A.
Marshall Cogan Purchase Fund

Massimo and Adriano Lagostina
Stockpot
1955. Stainless steel, 7¾" high
Manufacturer: Emilio Lagostina S.p.A., Italy
Phyllis B. Lambert Fund

Qq

Quartet

Ben Shahn
Portrait of Myself When Young
1943. Tempera on cardboard, 20 x 27⅞"
Purchase

Rr

Rocking chair

Gebrüder Thonet
Rocking Chair
1860. Bent beechwood and cane, 37½″ high
Manufacturer: Gebrüder Thonet, Austria
Gift of Café Nicholson

Ss

Soup

Andy Warhol
Campbell's Soup
1965. Oil silkscreened on canvas,
36⅛ x 24⅛"
Elizabeth Bliss Parkinson Fund

Andy Warhol
Campbell's Soup
1965. Oil silkscreened on canvas,
36⅛ x 24"
Philip Johnson Fund

Tt

Triangles

Ellsworth Kelly
Green-Blue
1968. Painted aluminum, 8'7½" x 9'4½" x 68½"
Susan Morse Hilles Fund

Uu

Umbrella

Fernand Léger
Umbrella and Bowler
1926. Oil on canvas, 50¼ x 38¾ "
A. Conger Goodyear Fund

Vase

Louis Comfort Tiffany
Vase
About 1900. Favrile glass, 20½″ high;
diameter at base, 4¾″
Manufacturer: Tiffany Studios, U.S.A.
Gift of Joseph H. Heil

Ww

Woman

Amedeo Modigliani
Anna Zborowska
1917. Oil on canvas, 51¼ x 32"
Lillie P. Bliss Collection

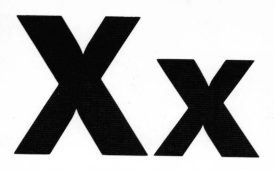

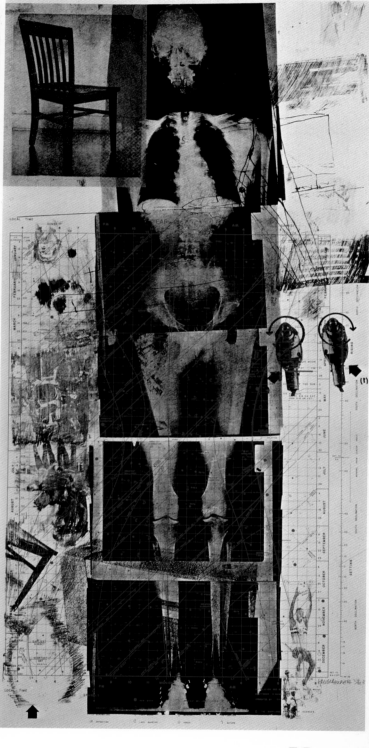

X-ray

Robert Rauschenberg
Booster
1967. Lithograph and serigraph,
printed in color, 71 9/16 x 35 1/8"
John B. Turner Fund

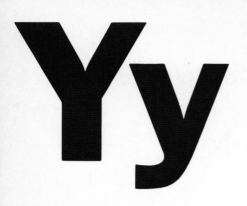

Yellow

Josef Albers
V from the portfolio *Midnight and Noon*
1964. Lithograph, printed in color, 15¾ x 15¾"
Gift of Kleiner, Bell & Co.

Zz

Zeros

Bridget Riley
PRINT 6
1965. Serigraph on plastic, 27 1/16 x 26"
Purchase

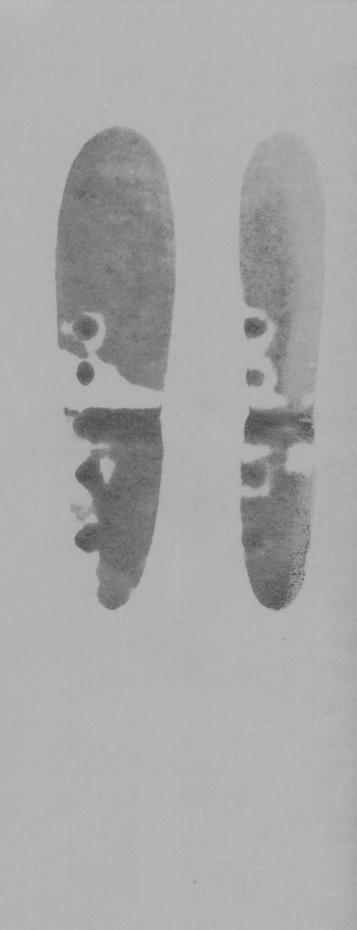

small stains
2/24